DODO EXTINCTUS · NUNQUAM OBLITURI DEM

Dodo Pad
ACADEMIC
2024-25

This Dodo Pad Academic is indodispensable. If found, please return to

NOTES

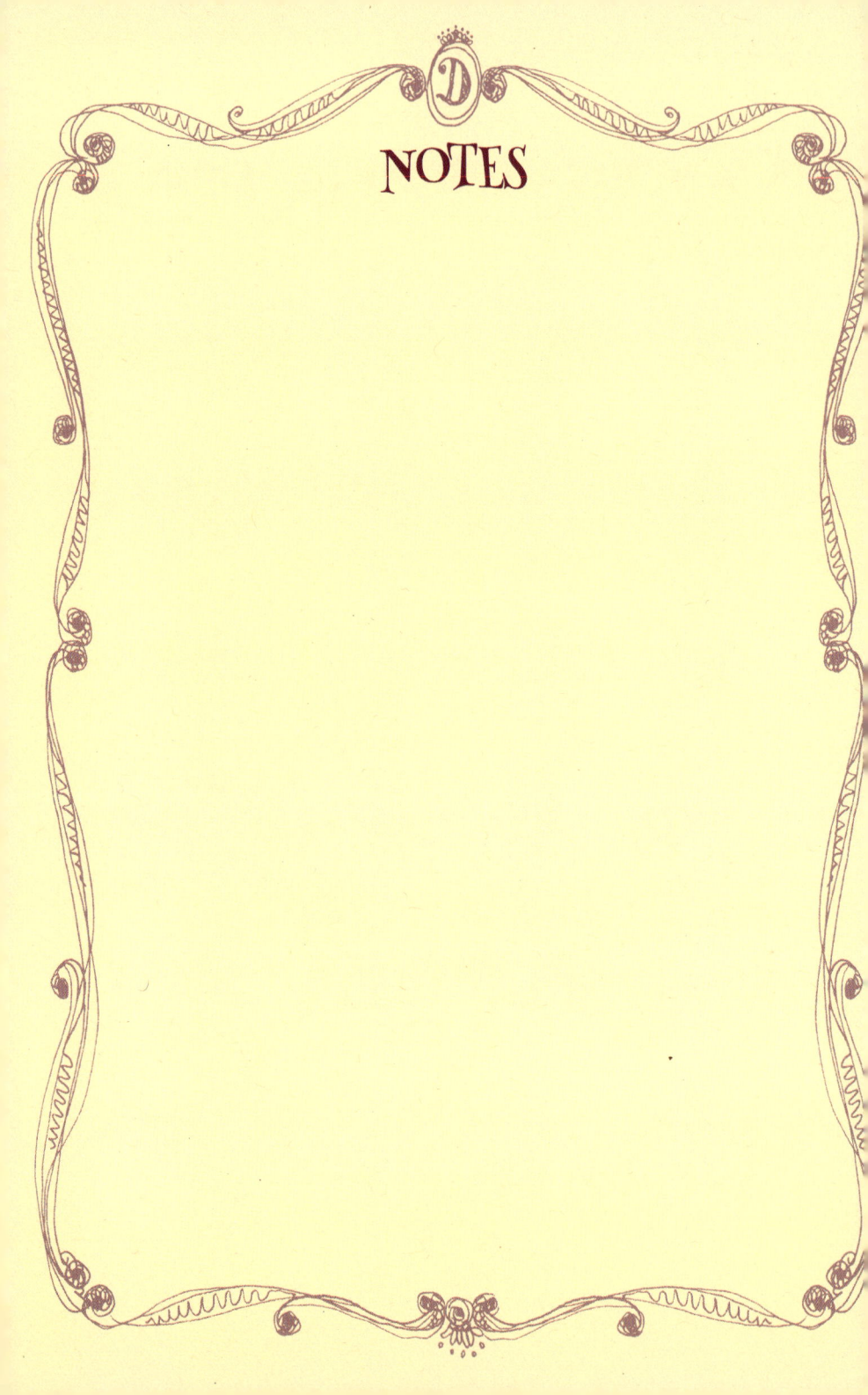

How to use your Dodo Pad Academic

MAY

	TO DO	Morning	Afternoon	Evening	DATES & DEADLINES
23 Monday	TV licence	9.00 lecture 4.00 presentation	5-7 yoga	Waitressing @ Rose & Crown	Jezmobile 07698 998 695
24 Tuesday	→ Photo developed - LIGHTBULBS - LADDER - book train PHONE TOM	DAY OFF	Tidy flat	Flat supper ✱ My turn	
25 Wednesday	write bread	10.00 lecture			Alice's 21st
26 Thursday	Fix curtain rail	10.30 Boiler	8.00 Hist. Soc. talk		HAND IN DISSERTATION PLAN Aaaahhhh!!!!!
27 Friday	RUBBISH DAY (Rupert's turn)	9.00 lecture 12. lecture	HAIRCUT 4pm "Slices"	FLAT PARTY ED'S	library books
28 Saturday	Jump start car ✱ PHONE HOME ✱	PIZZA Delivery 031 998 765		Belugas drinks 8pm. LIZ	Tutorial write-up - Reading theory & criticism
29 Sunday	Lie in		www.download music.com	waitress 6-12	Water cactus Feed goldfish Tom ketchup

Lord Dodo suggests that you that you may wish to use the boxes (as shown) or write across the feint dotted lines and use the space between the slanted lines at the top to break up the day as you so wish!

THIS 2024-25 YEAR

AUGUST	SEPTEMBER	OCTOBER	NOVEMBER	DECEMBER
M 5 12 19 26	M 2 9 16 23 30	M 7 14 21 28	M 4 11 18 25	M 2 9 16 23 30
T 6 13 20 27	T 3 10 17 24	T 1 8 15 22 29	T 5 12 19 26	T 3 10 17 24 31
W 7 14 21 28	W 4 11 18 25	W 2 9 16 23 30	W 6 13 20 27	W 4 11 18 25
T 1 8 15 22 29	T 5 12 19 26	T 3 10 17 24 31	T 7 14 21 28	T 5 12 19 26
F 2 9 16 23 30	F 6 13 20 27	F 4 11 18 25	F 1 8 15 22 29	F 6 13 20 27
S 3 10 17 24 31	S 7 14 21 28	S 5 12 19 26	S 2 9 16 23 30	S 7 14 21 28
S 4 11 18 25	S 1 8 15 22 29	S 6 13 20 27	S 3 10 17 24	S 1 8 15 22 29

JANUARY	FEBRUARY	MARCH	APRIL
M 6 13 20 27	M 3 10 17 24	M 3 10 17 24 31	M 7 14 21 28
T 7 14 21 28	T 4 11 18 25	T 4 11 18 25	T 1 8 15 22 29
W 1 8 15 22 29	W 5 12 19 26	W 5 12 19 26	W 2 9 16 23 30
T 2 9 16 23 30	T 6 13 20 27	T 6 13 20 27	T 3 10 17 24
F 3 10 17 24 31	F 7 14 21 28	F 7 14 21 28	F 4 11 18 25
S 4 11 18 25	S 1 8 15 22	S 1 8 15 22 29	S 5 12 19 26
S 5 12 19 26	S 2 9 16 23	S 2 9 16 23 30	S 6 13 20 27

MAY	JUNE	JULY	AUGUST	SEPTEMBER
M 5 12 19 26	M 2 9 16 23 30	M 7 14 21 28	M 4 11 18 25	M 1 8 15 22 29
T 6 13 20 27	T 3 10 17 24	T 1 8 15 22 29	T 5 12 19 26	T 2 9 16 23 30
W 7 14 21 28	W 4 11 18 25	W 2 9 16 23 30	W 6 13 20 27	W 3 10 17 24
T 1 8 15 22 29	T 5 12 19 26	T 3 10 17 24 31	T 7 14 21 28	T 4 11 18 25
F 2 9 16 23 30	F 6 13 20 27	F 4 11 18 25	F 1 8 15 22 29	F 5 12 19 26
S 3 10 17 24 31	S 7 14 21 28	S 5 12 19 26	S 2 9 16 23 30	S 6 13 20 27
S 4 11 18 25	S 1 8 15 22 29	S 6 13 20 27	S 3 10 17 24 31	S 7 14 21 28

Phases of the moon will be shown thus:
● New moon   ◐ 1st Quarter   ○ Full moon   ◑ 3rd Quarter

NEXT 2025-26 YEAR

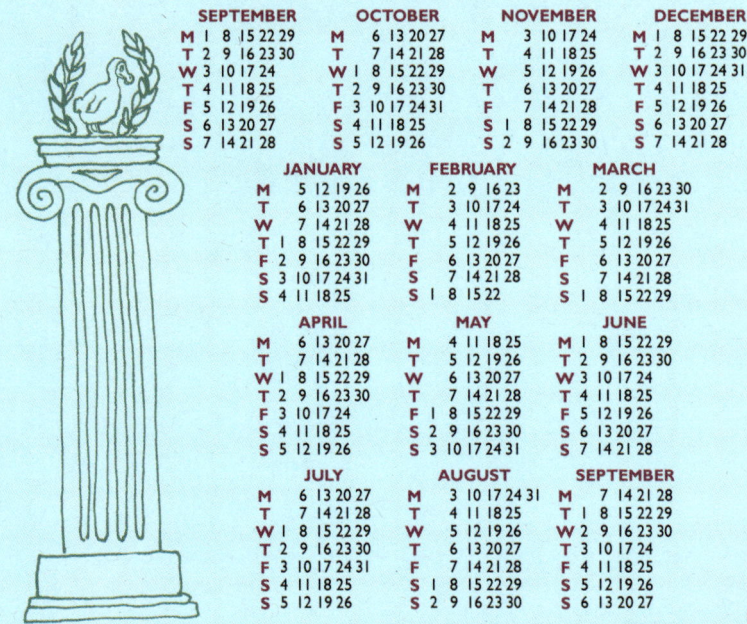

SEPTEMBER	OCTOBER	NOVEMBER	DECEMBER
M 1 8 15 22 29	M 6 13 20 27	M 3 10 17 24	M 1 8 15 22 29
T 2 9 16 23 30	T 7 14 21 28	T 4 11 18 25	T 2 9 16 23 30
W 3 10 17 24	W 1 8 15 22 29	W 5 12 19 26	W 3 10 17 24 31
T 4 11 18 25	T 2 9 16 23 30	T 6 13 20 27	T 4 11 18 25
F 5 12 19 26	F 3 10 17 24 31	F 7 14 21 28	F 5 12 19 26
S 6 13 20 27	S 4 11 18 25	S 1 8 15 22 29	S 6 13 20 27
S 7 14 21 28	S 5 12 19 26	S 2 9 16 23 30	S 7 14 21 28

JANUARY	FEBRUARY	MARCH
M 5 12 19 26	M 2 9 16 23	M 2 9 16 23 30
T 6 13 20 27	T 3 10 17 24	T 3 10 17 24 31
W 7 14 21 28	W 4 11 18 25	W 4 11 18 25
T 1 8 15 22 29	T 5 12 19 26	T 5 12 19 26
F 2 9 16 23 30	F 6 13 20 27	F 6 13 20 27
S 3 10 17 24 31	S 7 14 21 28	S 7 14 21 28
S 4 11 18 25	S 1 8 15 22	S 1 8 15 22 29

APRIL	MAY	JUNE
M 6 13 20 27	M 4 11 18 25	M 1 8 15 22 29
T 7 14 21 28	T 5 12 19 26	T 2 9 16 23 30
W 1 8 15 22 29	W 6 13 20 27	W 3 10 17 24
T 2 9 16 23 30	T 7 14 21 28	T 4 11 18 25
F 3 10 17 24	F 1 8 15 22 29	F 5 12 19 26
S 4 11 18 25	S 2 9 16 23 30	S 6 13 20 27
S 5 12 19 26	S 3 10 17 24 31	S 7 14 21 28

JULY	AUGUST	SEPTEMBER
M 6 13 20 27	M 3 10 17 24 31	M 7 14 21 28
T 7 14 21 28	T 4 11 18 25	T 1 8 15 22 29
W 1 8 15 22 29	W 5 12 19 26	W 2 9 16 23 30
T 2 9 16 23 30	T 6 13 20 27	T 3 10 17 24
F 3 10 17 24 31	F 7 14 21 28	F 4 11 18 25
S 4 11 18 25	S 1 8 15 22 29	S 5 12 19 26
S 5 12 19 26	S 2 9 16 23 30	S 6 13 20 27

TIME TABLE

	Monday	Tuesday	Wednesday	Thursday	Friday
L	U	N	C	H	

Notable Dates & Religious Festivals

Notable Dates	Religious Festivals	2024/25	2025/26
Father's Day (Aus)		1 September	7 September
Labor Day (US, Can)		2 September	1 September
Heritage Day (SA)		24 September	24 September
	Rosh Hashanah	3 October	23 September
	Yom Kippur	12 October	2 October
Columbus Day (US) Thanksgiving (Can)		14 October	13 October
BST ends (UK)		27 October	26 October
Bank Holiday (IRE)		28 October	27 October
	Halloween	31 October	31 October
	Diwali	1 November	20 October
Guy Fawkes' Night		5 November	5 November
Remembrance Sunday (UK)		10 November	9 November
Veterans Day (US) Remembrance Day (Can)		11 November	11 November
Thanksgiving (US)		28 November	27 November
Day of Reconciliation (SA)		16 December	16 December
	Christmas Day	25 December	25 December
	Hanukkah	26 December	15 December
Boxing Day (UK, SA, Aus, NZ)	St Stephen's Day (IRE)	26 December	26 December
New Year's Day (UK, US, IRE, SA, Aus, NZ)		1 January	1 January
New Year's Bank Holiday (Scot)		2 January	2 January
Martin Luther King Day (US)		20 January	19 January
Burn's Night		25 January	25 January
Australia Day		27 January	26 January
Chinese New Year		29 January	17 February
	St. Brigid's Day (IRE)	3 February	2 February
Waitangi Day		6 February	6 February
Presidents' Day (US)		17 February	16 February
	Ramadan begins	28 February	17 February
	Shrove Tuesday	4 March	17 February

Notable Dates & Religious Festivals

Notable Dates	Religious Festivals	2024/25	2025/26
Canberra Day (Aus) Commonwealth Day		10 March	9 March
Human Rights Day (SA)		21 March	21 March
	Mothering Sunday (UK, IRE)	30 March	15 March
BST begins (UK)		30 March	29 March
	Passover	13 April	2 April
	Good Friday	18 April	3 April
	Easter Sunday	20 April	5 April
	Easter Monday	21 April	6 April
Anzac Day (Aus, NZ)		25 April	27 April
Freedom Day (SA)		28 April	27 April
International Worker's Day (SA)		1 May	1 May
May Bank Holiday (UK, IRE)		5 May	4 May
Mother's Day (US, SA, Aus)		11 May	10 May
Victoria Day (Can)		19 May	18 May
Spring Bank Holiday (UK) Memorial Day (US)		26 May	25 May
Bank Holiday (IRE)		2 June	1 June
	Eid al Adha	7 June	27 May
Father's Day (UK, US, SA, Can)		15 June	21 June
Youth Day (SA)		16 June	16 June
Canada Day		1 July	1 July
Independence Day (US)		4 July	3 July
Public Holiday (N.Ireland)		14 July	13 July
Bastille Day		14 July	14 July
	Islamic New Year	26 July	17 June
Summer Bank Holiday (Scot, IRE)		4 August	3 August
National Women's Day (SA)		9 August	9 August
Summer Bank Holiday (UK)		25 August	31 August

When date falls on a Saturday or Sunday observed date is shown.
Where Religious Holidays are indicated, the first full day of the holiday is shown.
Public Holidays et al. This information is correct at time of going to press. The publishers can accept no responsibility for any errors.

FORWARD PLANNER 2024/25

September 2024

1 Su	17 T	
2 M	18 W	
3 T	19 Th	
4 W	20 F	
5 Th	21 S	
6 F	22 Su	
7 S	23 M	
8 Su	24 T	
9 M	25 W	
10 T	26 Th	
11 W	27 F	
12 Th	28 S	
13 F	29 Su	
14 S	30 M	
15 Su		
16 M		

October 2024

1 T	17 Th	
2 W	18 F	
3 Th	19 S	
4 F	20 Su	
5 S	21 M	
6 Su	22 T	
7 M	23 W	
8 T	24 Th	
9 W	25 F	
10 Th	26 S	
11 F	27 Su	
12 S	28 M	
13 Su	29 T	
14 M	30 W	
15 T	31 Th	
16 W		

November 2024

1 F	17 Su	
2 S	18 M	
3 Su	19 T	
4 M	20 W	
5 T	21 Th	
6 W	22 F	
7 Th	23 S	
8 F	24 Su	
9 S	25 M	
10 Su	26 T	
11 M	27 W	
12 T	28 Th	
13 W	29 F	
14 Th	30 S	
15 F		
16 S		

December 2024

1 Su	17 T	
2 M	18 W	
3 T	19 Th	
4 W	20 F	
5 Th	21 S	
6 F	22 Su	
7 S	23 M	
8 Su	24 T	
9 M	25 W	
10 T	26 Th	
11 W	27 F	
12 Th	28 S	
13 F	29 Su	
14 S	30 M	
15 Su	31 T	
16 M		

January 2025

1 W	17 F	
2 Th	18 S	
3 F	19 Su	
4 S	20 M	
5 Su	21 T	
6 M	22 W	
7 T	23 Th	
8 W	24 F	
9 Th	25 S	
10 F	26 Su	
11 S	27 M	
12 Su	28 T	
13 M	29 W	
14 T	30 Th	
15 W	31 F	
16 Th		

February 2025

1 S	17 M	
2 Su	18 T	
3 M	19 W	
4 T	20 Th	
5 W	21 F	
6 Th	22 S	
7 F	23 Su	
8 S	24 M	
9 Su	25 T	
10 M	26 W	
11 T	27 Th	
12 W	28 F	
13 Th		
14 F		
15 S		
16 Su		

FORWARDPLANNER FORWARDPLANNER FORWARDPL FOWARDPLANNER FORW 2024/25

MARCH 2025

1 S		17 M	
2 Su		18 T	
3 M		19 W	
4 T		20 Th	
5 W		21 F	
6 Th		22 S	
7 F		23 Su	
8 S		24 M	
9 Su		25 T	
10 M		26 W	
11 T		27 Th	
12 W		28 F	
13 Th		29 S	
14 F		30 Su	
15 S		31 M	
16 Su			

APRIL 2025

1 T		17 Th	
2 W		18 F	
3 Th		19 S	
4 F		20 Su	
5 S		21 M	
6 Su		22 T	
7 M		23 W	
8 T		24 Th	
9 W		25 F	
10 Th		26 S	
11 F		27 Su	
12 S		28 M	
13 Su		29 T	
14 M		30 W	
15 T			
16 W			

MAY 2025

1 Th		17 S	
2 F		18 Su	
3 S		19 M	
4 Su		20 T	
5 M		21 W	
6 T		22 Th	
7 W		23 F	
8 Th		24 S	
9 F		25 Su	
10 S		26 M	
11 Su		27 T	
12 M		28 W	
13 T		29 Th	
14 W		30 F	
15 Th		31 S	
16 F			

JUNE 2025

1 Su		17 T	
2 M		18 W	
3 T		19 Th	
4 W		20 F	
5 Th		21 S	
6 F		22 Su	
7 S		23 M	
8 Su		24 T	
9 M		25 W	
10 T		26 Th	
11 W		27 F	
12 Th		28 S	
13 F		29 Su	
14 S		30 M	
15 Su			
16 M			

JULY 2025

1 T		17 Th	
2 W		18 F	
3 Th		19 S	
4 F		20 Su	
5 S		21 M	
6 Su		22 T	
7 M		23 W	
8 T		24 Th	
9 W		25 F	
10 Th		26 S	
11 F		27 Su	
12 S		28 M	
13 Su		29 T	
14 M		30 W	
15 T		31 Th	
16 W			

AUGUST 2025

1 F		17 Su	
2 S		18 M	
3 Su		19 T	
4 M		20 W	
5 T		21 Th	
6 W		22 F	
7 Th		23 S	
8 F		24 Su	
9 S		25 M	
10 Su		26 T	
11 M		27 W	
12 T		28 Th	
13 W		29 F	
14 Th		30 S	
15 F		31 Su	
16 S			

Lord Dodo's newest member of the kitchen staff, a charming young Greek fellow, clearly needs a little more training in the technique of dishwasher loading...

July–August 2024

Week 31

29 Monday

30 Tuesday

31 Wednesday

1 Thursday

2 Friday

3 Saturday

1913 Death of Josephine Cochrane, inventor of the first commercially successful dishwasher

4 Sunday

Young Lady Wisteria Dodo was amused to read this inscription in a churchyard in Bushey, Hertfordshire—but rejoiced in how the much the status of women has changed in the intervening century...

† R.I.P. A TIRED WOMAN

Here lies a poor woman who always was tired,
For she lived in a place where help wasn't hired,
Her last words on earth were, 'Dear friends, I am going,
Where washing ain't done, nor cooking nor sewing,
And everything there is exact to my wishes,
For there they don't eat, there's no washing dishes,
I'll be where loud anthems will always be ringing
(But having no voice, I'll be out of the singing).
Don't mourn for me now, don't grieve for me never,
For I'm going to do nothing for ever and ever.'

AUGUST 2024

Week 32

5 Monday — Summer Bank Holiday SCOT, IRE

6 Tuesday

7 Wednesday

8 Thursday

9 Friday — National Woman's Day SA

10 Saturday

11 Sunday

Recent DNA testing has revealed that Iris, Dowager Lady Dodo, is 80% Irish.

An extract from the Dodo family tree, on display to the public in the Long Gallery, Dodo Towers.

August 2024

Week 33

12 Monday

13 Tuesday — Obon — 1838 Death of John Farmer, known as the founder of systematic genealogy in America

14 Wednesday

15 Thursday

16 Friday

17 Saturday

18 Sunday

As Mrs Khan tied up the bottom of the family ger for the annual spring-clean, little did she know that she was using a primitive form of *ger-conditioning*.

August 2024

Week 34

19 Monday

20 Tuesday

21 Wednesday

22 Thursday

23 Friday

24 Saturday

25 Sunday

1227 Death of Genghis Khan after a fall from his horse

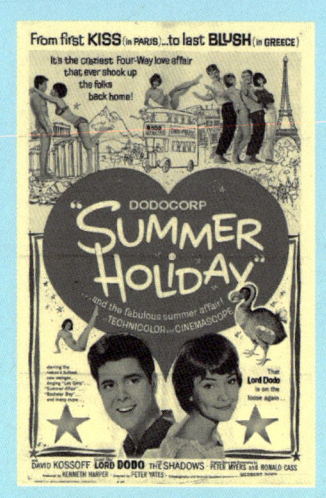

Calling all Dodopadlers!
Which drawing of the Dodo from this year's Dodo Pad would you like to see included on next year's cover among the other portraits? His Lordship would love to hear from you. Suggestions please to
info@dodopad.com

AUGUST / SEPTEMBER 2024

Week 35

26 Monday — Summer Bank Holiday UK   Krishna Janmashtami

27 Tuesday

28 Wednesday

29 Thursday

30 Friday

31 Saturday

1 Sunday — Father's Day AUS

Art historians may dispute the authenticity of this, a pearl among the many treasures in the Long Gallery at Dodo Towers, but Lord Dodo is adamant that it is the real McCoy.

September 2024

Week 36

2 Monday — Labor Day US & CAN — Pierce Your Ears Day

3 Tuesday

4 Wednesday

5 Thursday

6 Friday

7 Saturday

8 Sunday

Most dinosaurs couldn't read...now they are extinct.

Thank goodness the Thesaurus survived!

September 2024

Week 37

9 Monday

10 Tuesday

11 Wednesday

12 Thursday — 1869 Death of Peter Mark Roget

13 Friday

14 Saturday

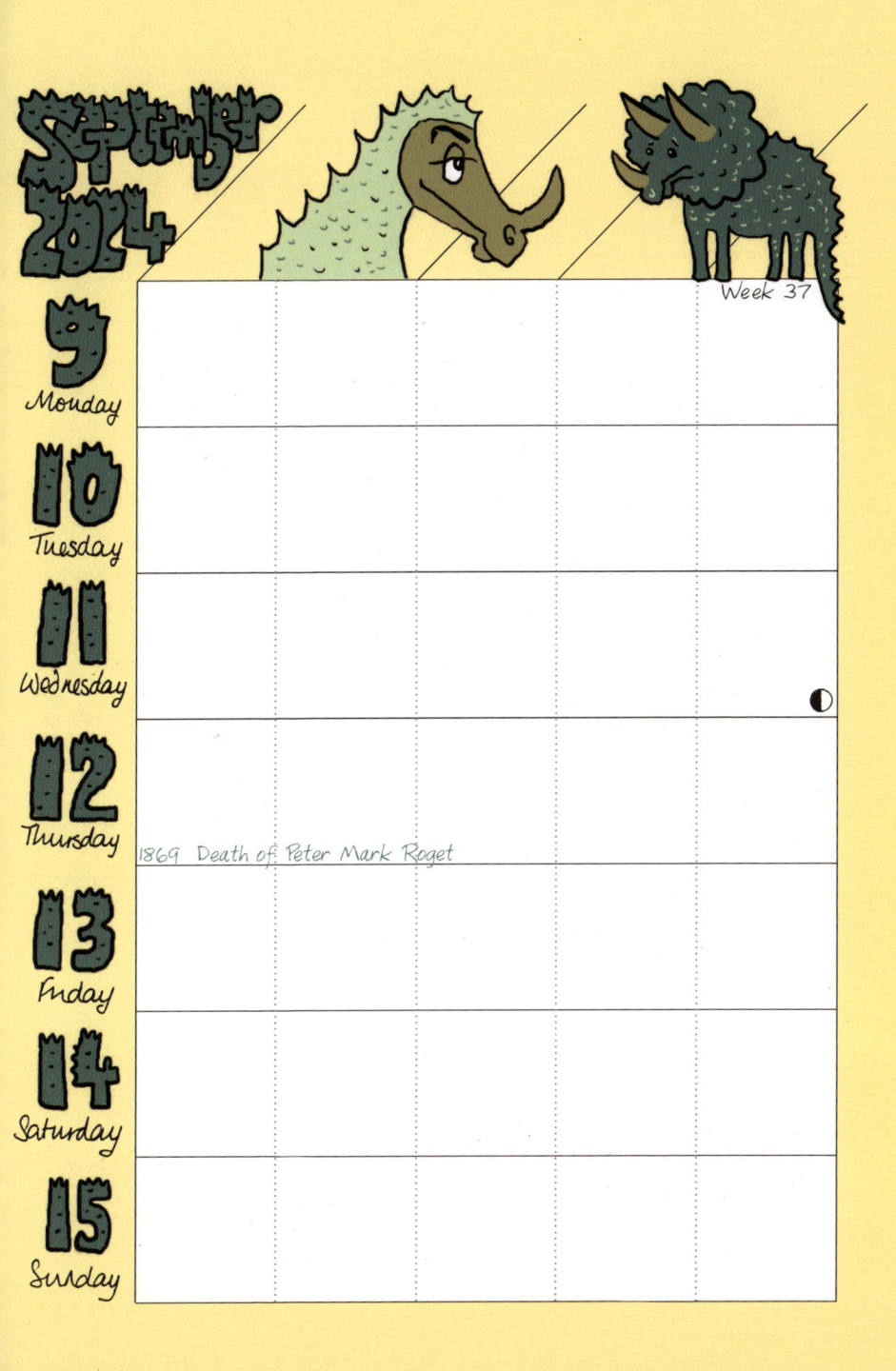

15 Sunday

PIE SHACK
MEAT PIES $3
VEG PIES $2

BARBADOS

PIE SHACK
MEAT PIES $2.75
VEG PIES $2.25

JAMAICA

The Pie Rates of the Caribbean

SEPTEMBER 2024

Week 38

16 Monday

17 Tuesday

18 Wednesday

19 Thursday — Talk Like a Pirate Day

20 Friday

21 Saturday

22 Sunday — Autumn Equinox

Don't panic, it's only September - but it is time to consider what Dodo Diary Produce you might like to order as Christmas gifts. Have a look at our full range at www.dodopad.com

SANTA SCHOOL CLASS TIMETABLE

	MONDAY	TUESDAY	WEDNESDAY	THURSDAY	FRIDAY
9 am	ELVES Terms of hire & working conditions	KNOW YOUR REINDEER (advanced)	SLEIGH Team-building session	HO HO Honing technique	Gift wrapping (intermediate)
11 am	SAT NAV for Santas	Beard Hygiene	Bell Jingling (beginners)	Chimney Climbing Practice	The Milk & Biscuit Diet

September 2024

Week 39

23 Monday

24 Tuesday
Heritage Day SA ◐

25 Wednesday

26 Thursday

27 Friday
1937 A school for Santa Clauses opens in Albion, New York

28 Saturday

29 Sunday
DST begins NZ

"Have you always been a proofreader?"

"No – it's just a phrase I'm going through."

September / October 2024

Week 40

30 Monday

1 Tuesday — 2019 Seal of Charter granted to Society of Proofreaders & Editors

2 Wednesday ●

3 Thursday — Rosh Hashanah

4 Friday

5 Saturday

6 Sunday — DST begins AUS

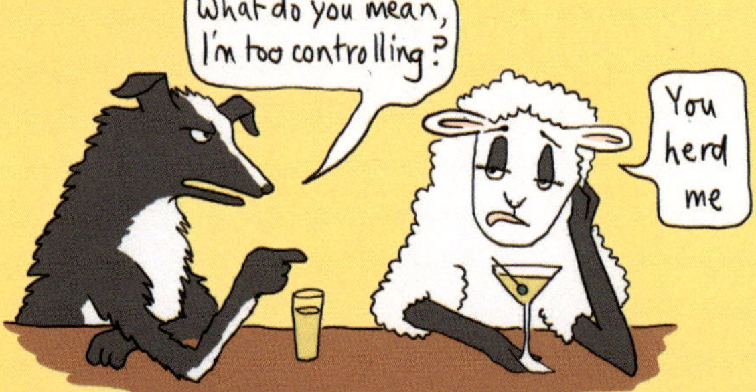
What do you mean, I'm too controlling?
You herd me

October 2024

Week 41

7 Monday — Labour Day AUS   1943 Release of the movie 'Lassie Come Home'

8 Tuesday

9 Wednesday

10 Thursday

11 Friday

12 Saturday — Yom Kippur   Dasara

13 Sunday

EMOTIONAL TIES

- I'm going to cry
- Sob sob
- What about me?
- Boo hoo
- Don't start me off

October 2024

Week 42

14 Monday — Columbus Day US   Thanksgiving CAN

15 Tuesday

16 Wednesday

17 Thursday

18 Friday — International Necktie Day

19 Saturday

20 Sunday

Just because nobody complains doesn't mean all parachutes are perfect.
Benny Hill

October 2024

21 Monday

22 Tuesday

1797 World's first parachute jump (from a hot air balloon) by André-Jacques Garnerin

23 Wednesday

24 Thursday

25 Friday

26 Saturday

27 Sunday

Week 43

BST ends

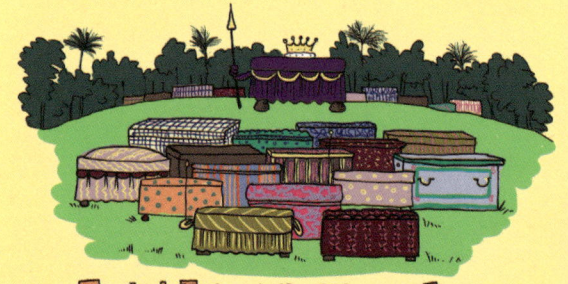

The Lost Tribe of the Ottoman Empire

October / November 2024

Week 44

28 Monday — Holiday ROI | Labour Day NZ

29 Tuesday

30 Wednesday

31 Thursday — Hallowe'en

1 Friday — Diwali | 1922 Formal dissolution of the Ottoman Empire by the Grand National Assembly of Turkey

2 Saturday

3 Sunday — DST ends USA

Dodubious Information

A busker whom Lord Dodo used to see on his way to the City told him that he'd trained his dog to play the trumpet on the Underground. He said he went from Barking to Tooting in just over an hour.

November 2024

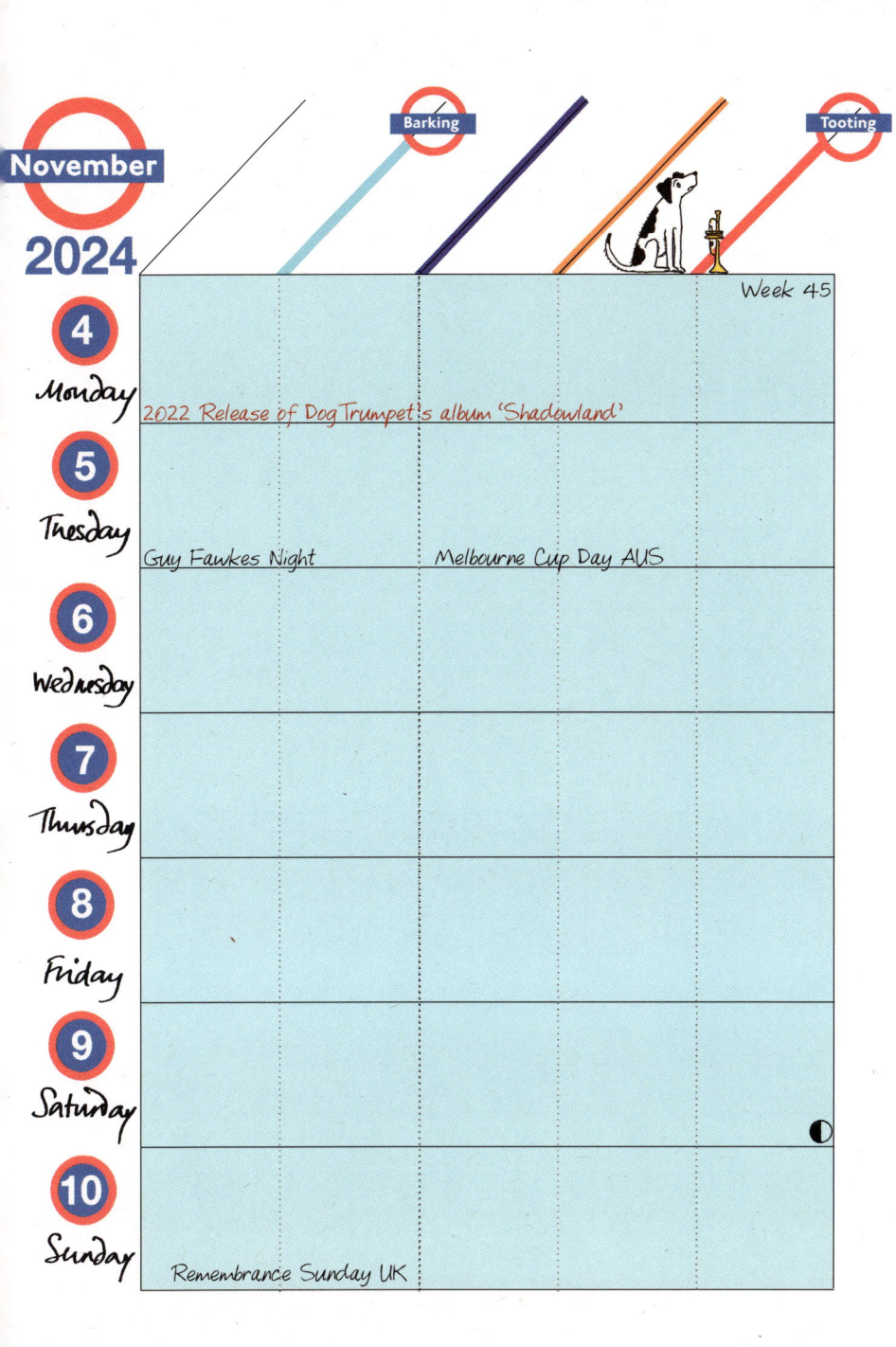

Week 45

4 Monday
2022 Release of Dog Trumpet's album 'Shadowland'

5 Tuesday
Guy Fawkes Night — Melbourne Cup Day AUS

6 Wednesday

7 Thursday

8 Friday

9 Saturday

10 Sunday
Remembrance Sunday UK

It is better to have loafed and lost, than never to have loafed at all. *James Thurber*

November 2024

11 Monday — Veterans' Day US   Remembrance Day CAN

12 Tuesday

13 Wednesday — World Kindness Day

14 Thursday

15 Friday — Guru Nanak's Birthday ○

16 Saturday

17 Sunday — Feast Day of St Elizabeth of Hungary, patron saint of bakers

Week 46

His Lordship prides himself on his fluency in many of the languages within his pangalactic publishing empire but, embarrassingly, he is struggling to master Mandarin. This is as far as he's got... **HELLO**

NOVEMBER 2024

Week 47

- **18 Monday**
- **19 Tuesday**
- **20 Wednesday**
- **21 Thursday**
- **22 Friday**
- **23 Saturday**
- **24 Sunday**

Weekend of annual Mountain Mandarin Festival, Placer County, California

Lord Dodo is always on the lookout for something special when it comes to family holidays, places that will spark his offspring's interest and have them scribbling furiously in their journals to record every magic moment. Sadly the vacation destinations he organised for them last year, though involving travel over three continents, did not go down so well. Here's little Lady Wisteria Dodo with her recollections of the trip...

OUR HOLIDAYS 2022
Papa took us to
BLAND
DULL
BORING
THE TRINITY
NSW Australia
Perth, Scotland
Oregon, USA
OF TEDIUM

NOVEMBER DECEMBER 2024

BLAND SHIRE NEW SOUTH WALES

DULL Perth & Kinross SCOTLAND

BORING OREGON Welcomes you!

Week 48

25 Monday

26 Tuesday

27 Wednesday

28 Thursday — Thanksgiving USA

29 Friday

30 Saturday

1 Sunday — 1932 Death of William H Boring, American Union Soldier, who founded the town of Boring, Oregon in 1874

MY THEORY OF EVOLUTION IS THAT DARWIN WAS ADOPTED   STEVEN WRIGHT

December 2024

Week 49

2 Monday — St Andrew's Day (obs)

1960 Paleoanthropologist Louis Leakey discovered a 1.4 million-year-old Homo Erectus in Olduvai Gorge, Tanzania.

3 Tuesday

4 Wednesday

5 Thursday

6 Friday

7 Saturday

8 Sunday

FROSTY THE SNOWMAN
PICKS HIS NOSE

December 2024

Week 50

9 Monday — 1965 Charlie Brown Christmas Special first aired on TV

10 Tuesday

11 Wednesday

12 Thursday

13 Friday

14 Saturday

15 Sunday

The Dodo Pad is indodispensable for keeping busy Sugar Plum Fairies *en pointe* throughout the year.

I'm bored stiff by ballet. I can't bear those muscular white legs like unbaked plaited loaves, and I get quite hysterical every time one of the women sticks out her leg at right angles, and the man suddenly grabs it and walks round in a circle as though he were opening a tin.
Jilly Cooper

December 2024

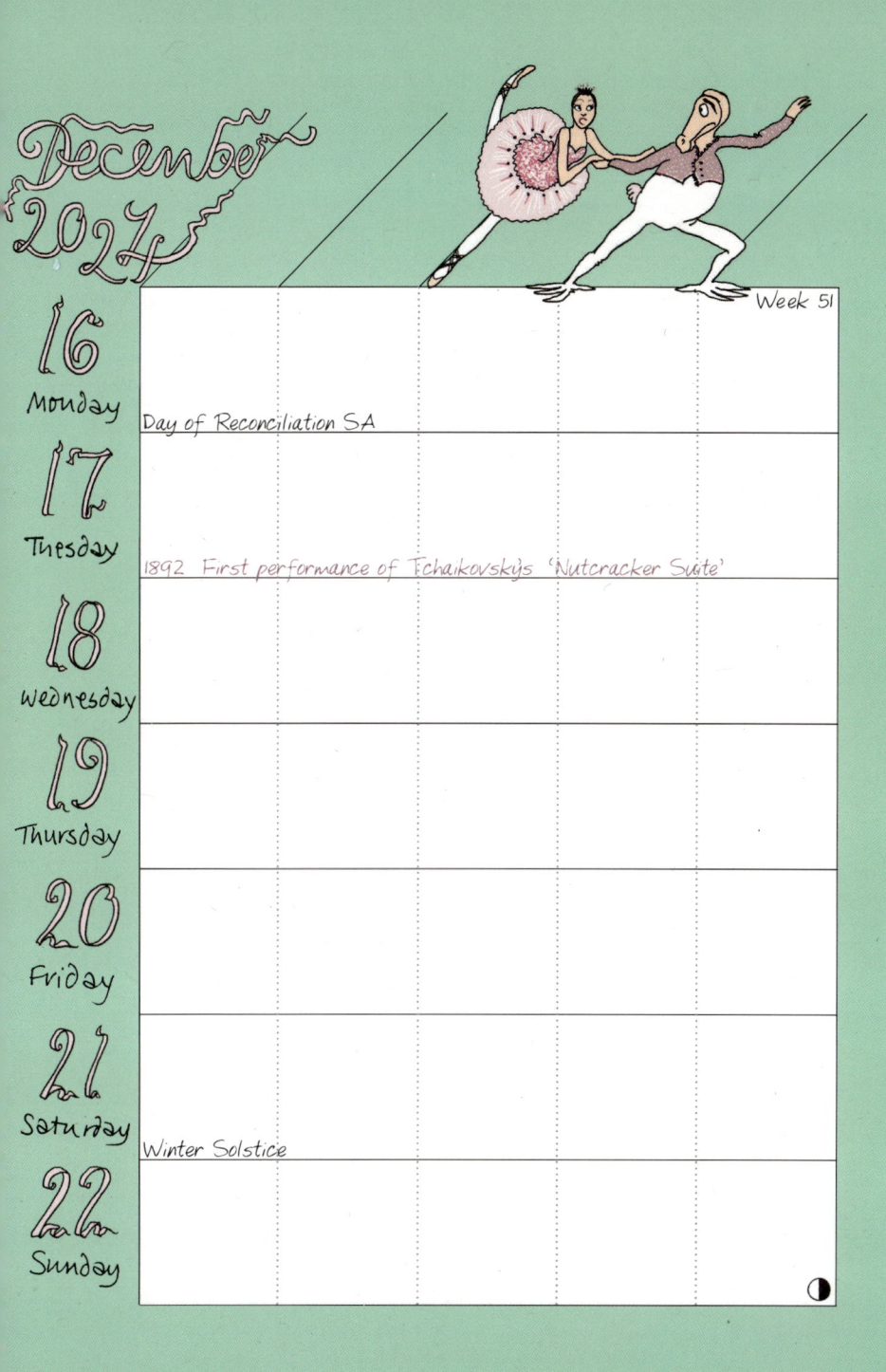

Week 51

16 Monday — Day of Reconciliation SA

17 Tuesday — 1892 First performance of Tchaikovsky's 'Nutcracker Suite'

18 Wednesday

19 Thursday

20 Friday

21 Saturday — Winter Solstice

22 Sunday

Little Lady Luiza Dodo is dodevoted to Furball, her pet moggie, and they both love decorating the big tree in the Great Hall at Dodo Towers. She has compiled a Christmas playlist to divert Furball from the carnage he can sometimes wreak around the decorations; here are some of their favourite song titles...

I saw Mommy Hiss at Santa Claus
Have yourself a Furry Little Christmas
O Come All Ye Fishful
The First Miaow
Wreck the Halls
Jingle Balls
Silent Mice

His Lordship would be dodelighted to receive any other seasonal aural gems. A free Dodo Pad will wing its way to anyone who makes it on to Lady Luiza's published playlist in the future. Email to info@dodopad.com or share on social media. #dodopad

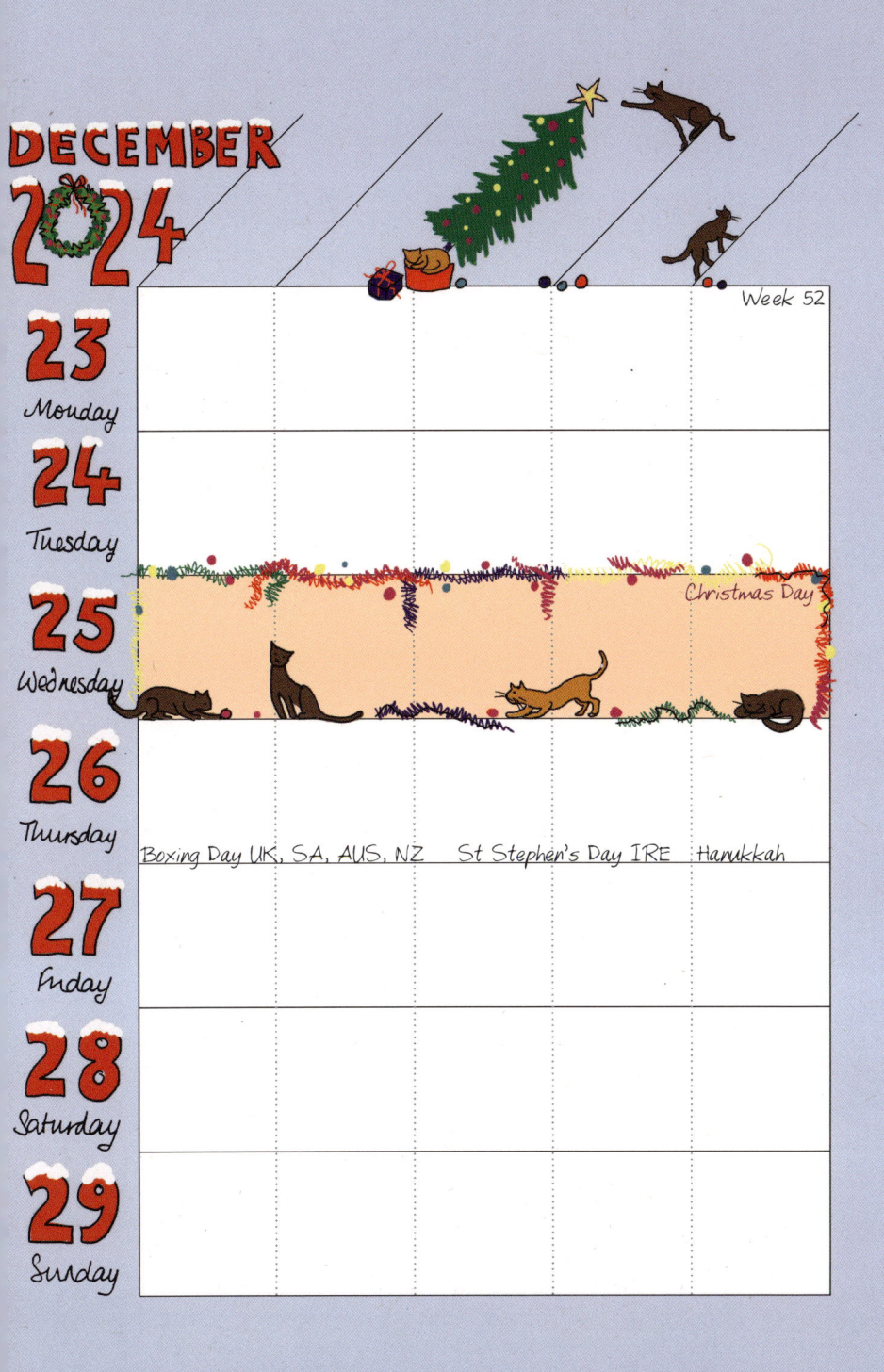

DECEMBER 2024

Week 52

23 Monday

24 Tuesday

25 Wednesday — Christmas Day

26 Thursday — Boxing Day UK, SA, AUS, NZ   St Stephen's Day IRE   Hanukkah

27 Friday

28 Saturday

29 Sunday

NOT ENTIRELY DODODUBIOUS INFORMATION...
Catherine de Medici liked to ride side-saddle, so to protect her modesty on windy days, wore undergarments later to be known as knickers, and is generally regarded as the first European woman to wear them. (And of course she would also have felt undressed without her Dodo Pad.)

December 2024 / January 2025

Week 1

30 Monday

31 Tuesday

1 Wednesday
New Year's Day UK, IRE, US, AUS, NZ

2 Thursday
Bank Holiday SCOT

3 Friday

4 Saturday

5 Sunday

1589 Death of Catherine de Medici, Queen of France

After an exhausting season of Christmas cooking at Dodo Towers, Cook takes a well-earned break with her family...

Janvier 2025

Week 2

6 Monday

7 Tuesday

8 Wednesday

9 Thursday

10 Friday

11 Saturday

12 Sunday

1833 Death of chef Marie Antoine Carême

St Anthony the Abbot consults the indodispensable Dodo Pad Book for Cooks for his favourite pizza recipe.

January 2025

Week 3

13 Monday

14 Tuesday

15 Wednesday

16 Thursday

17 Friday — Feast Day of St Anthony the Abbot, patron saint of pizza

18 Saturday

19 Sunday

now is the winter of our...

JANUARY 2025

	Week 4
20 Monday	Martin Luther King Day US
21 Tuesday	◐
22 Wednesday	
23 Thursday	
24 Friday	1908 'Scouting for Boys' first published
25 Saturday	Burns Night
26 Sunday	

There was a young man from Peru
Whose limerick stopped at line two.

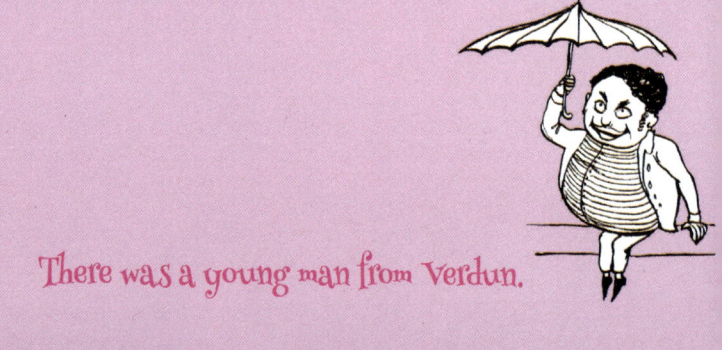

There was a young man from Verdun.

January
February
2025

Week 5

27 Monday — Australia Day (obs)

28 Tuesday

29 Wednesday — Chinese New Year   1888 Death of Edward Lear

30 Thursday

31 Friday

1 Saturday

2 Sunday

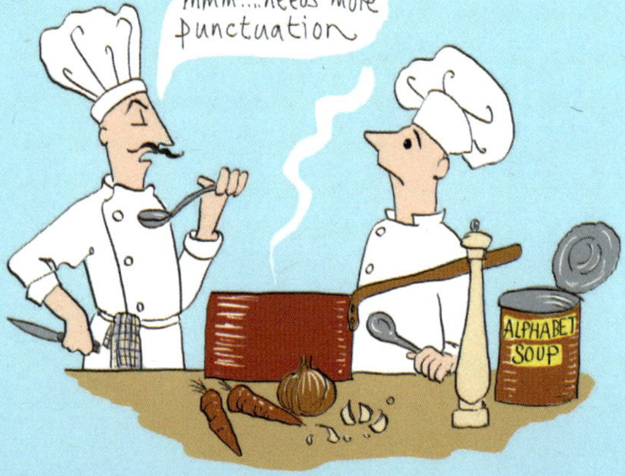
mmm....needs more punctuation
ALPHABET SOUP

February 2025

Week 6

3 Monday — St Brigid's Day IRE (obs)

4 Tuesday — National Home-Made Soup Day

5 Wednesday

6 Thursday — Waitangi Day NZ

7 Friday

8 Saturday

9 Sunday

I'm **WILD** about you!
Be my Valentine...

FEBRUARY 2025

Week 7

10 MONDAY

11 TUESDAY

12 WEDNESDAY

13 THURSDAY

14 FRIDAY — Valentine's Day

15 SATURDAY

16 SUNDAY

Engraved on the collar of a dog which I gave to His Royal Highness Frederick, Prince of Wales

I am his Highness' dog at Kew
Pray tell me, sir, whose dog are you?

Alexander Pope

February 2025

Week 8

17 Monday — President's Day US

18 Tuesday

19 Wednesday

20 Thursday ◐

21 Friday

22 Saturday

23 Sunday — International Dog Biscuit Appreciation Day

Struggling actor, Leonard Nimoy, when offered a part in Star Trek, couldn't believe his ears.

FEBRUARY MARCH 2025

24 Monday

25 Tuesday

26 Wednesday

27 Thursday
2015 Death of Leonard Nimoy, best known as Mr Spock in Star Trek

28 Friday
Ramadan begins

1 Saturday
St David's Day

2 Sunday

Week 9

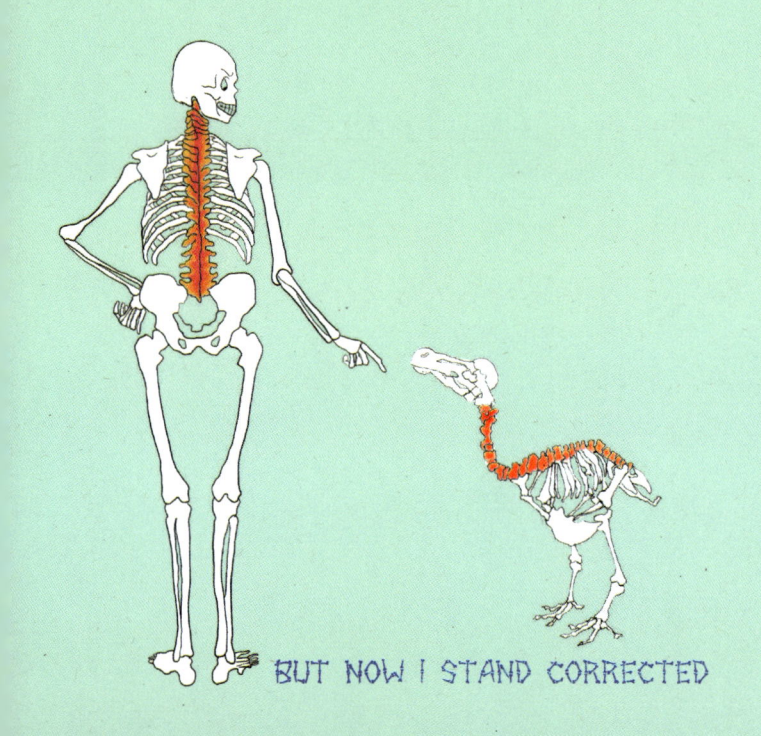

INITIALLY I DIDN'T THINK MY CHIROPRACTOR WAS ANY GOOD

BUT NOW I STAND CORRECTED

MARCH 2025

Week 10

3 Monday

4 Tuesday — Shrove Tuesday

5 Wednesday — Ash Wednesday

6 Thursday

7 Friday — Birth of D.D. Palmer, founder of Chiropractic

8 Saturday — International Women's Day

9 Sunday — DST begins US

CEDAR! BEWARE THE ADZE of MARCH

MARCH
MMXXV

Week 11

10 Monday — Canberra Day   Commonwealth Day

11 Tuesday

12 Wednesday

13 Thursday

14 Friday — Holi   ○

15 Saturday — The Ides of March... 1820 Maine, The Pine Tree State, joined the Union

16 Sunday

WHAT DOES WINNIE THE POOH CALL HIS SIGNIFICANT OTHER?

HUNNY

MARCH 2025

Week 12

17 Monday — St Patrick's Day

18 Tuesday

19 Wednesday

20 Thursday — Spring Equinox

21 Friday — Human Rights Day SA

22 Saturday

23 Sunday — World Bear Day

Homing pigeon GI Joe saved the lives of British troops and the inhabitants of Calvi Vecchia, Italy. The village had been liberated far quicker than expected. Earlier, an American air raid had been scheduled to subdue the German positions. The Allied advance had been so rapid that there was now a danger of being caught in 'friendly fire'. Unable to transmit a message, GI Joe was released as a last resort. In 20 minutes he flew 20 miles to the airbase and arrived just in time to stop the raid. He was awarded the Dickin Medal for gallantry in November 1946, the animal equivalent of the Victoria Cross.

March 2025

Week 13

24 Monday
1943 Birth of homing pigeon GI Joe

25 Tuesday

26 Wednesday

27 Thursday

28 Friday

29 Saturday

30 Sunday
BST begins
Eid al-Fitr   Mothering Sunday UK & IRE

Here lies the body
of Mary Ann Lowder.
She burst while drinking
a seidlitz powder.
Called from this world
to her heavenly rest,
She should have waited
till it effervesced.

Anon

MARCH / APRIL 2025

ALKA SELTZER

Week 14

31 Monday

1 Tuesday
1929 Death of Dr Franklin Lawrence Miles, founder of the company that invented Alka Seltzer

2 Wednesday

3 Thursday

4 Friday

5 Saturday

6 Sunday
DST ends AUS, NZ

I was asked to leave the choir when I tried to sing the high parts...

...they said I was a treblemaker

April 2025

Week 15

7 MONDAY

8 TUESDAY

9 WEDNESDAY

10 THURSDAY

11 FRIDAY

12 SATURDAY

13 SUNDAY

Passover   1742 First performance of Handel's Messiah

Dear Lord, the day of eggs is here...
Amanda McKittrick Ros

Perfidious Albumen

APRIL 2025

14 Monday — Baisakhi

15 Tuesday

16 Wednesday

17 Thursday

18 Friday — Good Friday

19 Saturday

20 Sunday — Easter Sunday

Week 16

Nice to see thou, to see thou, nice.
— BRUCE FORSOOTH

April 2025

Week 17

21 Monday — Easter Monday

22 Tuesday

23 Wednesday — St George's Day   Talk like Shakespeare Day

24 Thursday

25 Friday — ANZAC Day

26 Saturday

27 Sunday

Dodododubious Information

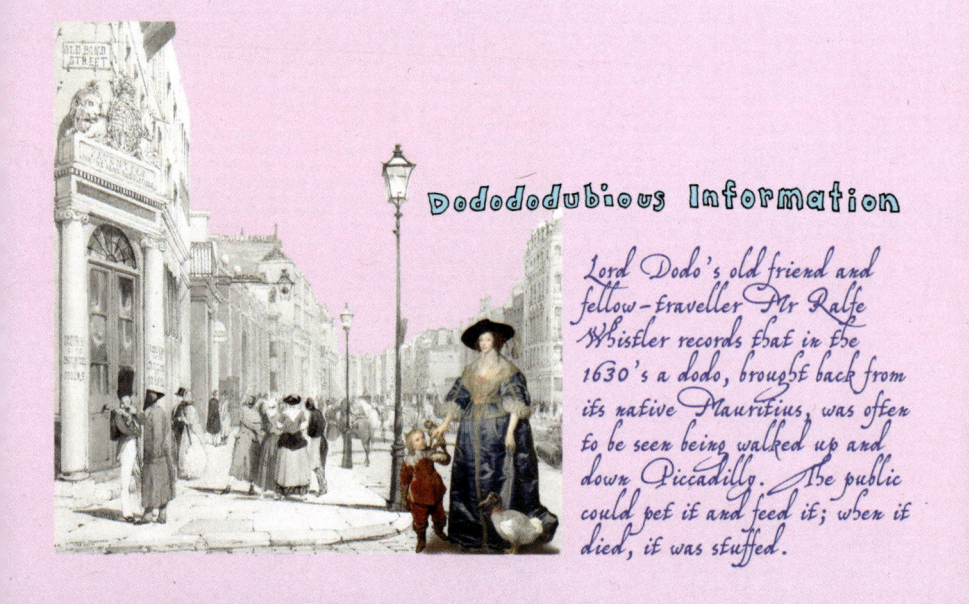

Lord Dodo's old friend and fellow-traveller Mr Ralfe Whistler records that in the 1630's a dodo, brought back from its native Mauritius, was often to be seen being walked up and down Piccadilly. The public could pet it and feed it; when it died, it was stuffed.

APRIL / MAY 2025

Week 18

28 Monday — Freedom Day SA (obs)

29 Tuesday — 2023 Death of celebrated dodoist Ralfe Whistler

30 Wednesday

1 Thursday — International Workers' Day SA

2 Friday

3 Saturday

4 Sunday

The first board meeting at Dodocorp HQ...

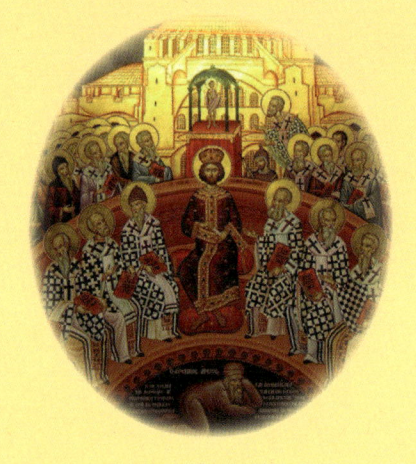

You can't teach an old dogma new tricks
Dorothy Parker

MAY 2025

Week 19

5 Monday — Bank Holiday UK, IRE   325AD Council of Nicea began in May of this year

6 Tuesday

7 Wednesday

8 Thursday

9 Friday

10 Saturday

11 Sunday — Mother's Day US, AUS, SA

The camel: did you ever see anything that reminded you so much of a dowager duchess studying the hoi polloi through a gold-rimmed lorgnette?

Fyfe Robinson

MAY 2025

12 Monday
13 Tuesday
14 Wednesday
15 Thursday
16 Friday
17 Saturday
18 Sunday

Week 20

Visakha Puja Day

1856 The first camels to be used for commercial purposes in the US arrived in Indianola, Texas

Anatomy of a Bumble Bee

BLEBEE

BUM

May 2025

							Week 21

19 Monday
Victoria Day

20 Tuesday
World Bee Day ◐

21 Wednesday

22 Thursday

23 Friday

24 Saturday

25 Sunday

What exotic birds, native to Cornwall, fly over the countryside singing light opera arias?

The Parrots of Penzance

May / June 2025

Week 22

26 Monday — Spring Bank Holiday UK   Memorial Day US

27 Tuesday

28 Wednesday ●

29 Thursday

30 Friday — 1911 Death of W. S Gilbert

31 Saturday

Sunday

ROCK CLIMBING

I'D TRY THIS IF ONLY I WAS A LITTLE BOULDER...

JUNE 2025

Week 23

2 Monday

3 Tuesday
2017 Alex Honnold made the first free solo ascent of El Capitan, Yosemite ◐

4 Wednesday

5 Thursday

6 Friday

7 Saturday
Eid al-Adha

8 Sunday

> Never commit murder. A gentleman should never do anything he cannot talk about at dinner.
>
> — Oscar Wilde

June 2025

Week 24

9 Monday — King's Birthday AUS

10 Tuesday

11 Wednesday ○

12 Thursday

13 Friday — 1949 Premiére of the movie 'Kind Hearts and Coronets'

14 Saturday

15 Sunday — Father's Day UK, US, CAN, SA

> I'm sick of war for many reasons,
> Three of them will do:
> It's 1815,
> I am French
> And this is Waterloo.
> — Mel Brooks

JUNE 2025

Week 25

16 Monday — Youth Day SA

17 Tuesday

18 Wednesday — 1815 Battle of Waterloo ☽

19 Thursday

20 Friday

21 Saturday — Summer Solstice

22 Sunday

Dodubious Information
An outbreak of St John's Dance was an annual event when the consignment of next year's Dodo Pads arrived in the village. Let joy be unconfined!

June 2025

23 Monday

24 Tuesday

25 Wednesday

26 Thursday

27 Friday

28 Saturday

29 Sunday

Week 26

1374 A huge outbreak of St John's Dance (also called St Vitus' Dance), began in Aachen

How do you calculate the circumference of a sheep?

Shepherd's π

June / July 2025

Week 27

30 Monday

1 Tuesday — Canada Day

2 Wednesday

3 Thursday

4 Friday — Independence Day US

5 Saturday — 1996 Birth of Dolly, the world's first cloned sheep

6 Sunday

'Can you dance?' said the girl. Lancelot gave a short, amused laugh. He was a man who never let his left hip know what his right hip was doing.
P. G. Wodehouse

July 2025

Week 28

7 Monday

8 Tuesday

9 Wednesday
1907 Première of The Zeigfeld Follies at the Olympia Theatre, New York

10 Thursday
Asalha Puja Day ○

11 Friday

12 Saturday

13 Sunday

MOWNA LISA

July 2025

Week 29

14 Monday — Holiday NI — Bastille Day

15 Tuesday — 1542 Death of Lisa del Giaconda, model for the Mona Lisa

16 Wednesday

17 Thursday

18 Friday — Nelson Mandela Day SA

19 Saturday

20 Sunday

ELECTRIC FENCE

ACOUSTIC FENCE

July 2025

Week 30

21 Monday

22 Tuesday

23 Wednesday

24 Thursday

25 Friday

1965 Bob Dylan was booed for performing his first set with an electric guitar

26 Saturday

Islamic New Year

27 Sunday

Darling - don't forget to order next year's Dodo Pad

JULY
AUGUST
MMXXV

Week 31

28 Monday

29 Tuesday

30 Wednesday

31 Thursday

1 Friday
10 BC Birth of the Roman Emperor Claudius

2 Saturday

3 Sunday

Peotry is sissy stuff that rhymes.
Weedy people say la and fie and
swoon when they see a bunch of
daffodils.
Aktually there is only one piece of
peotry in the english language.
The Brook
i come from haunts of coot and hern
i make a sudden sally
and-er-hem-er-hem-the fern
to bicker down a valley
Geoffrey Willans and Ronald Searle
'Down with Skool'

August 2025

Week 32

4 Monday — Summer Bank Holiday SCOT, IRE

5 Tuesday

6 Wednesday — 1809 Birth of Alfred, Lord Tennyson, Poet Laureate

7 Thursday

8 Friday

9 Saturday — National Women's Day SA

10 Sunday

August 2025

Week 33

11 Monday

12 Tuesday

13 Wednesday — Obon   2022 The first Tamil Nadu Kite Festival began at Mamallapuram

14 Thursday

15 Friday

16 Saturday — Krishna Janmashtani ◑

17 Sunday

The fastest means of communication in
the Philippines are telephone, telegram,
and tell a nun.
Cardinal Sin of the Philippines.

August 2025

Week 34

08 Monday

09 Tuesday

20 Wednesday — 1896 The Eriksson brothers submitted a patent for the first dial telephone

21 Thursday

22 Friday

23 Saturday

24 Sunday

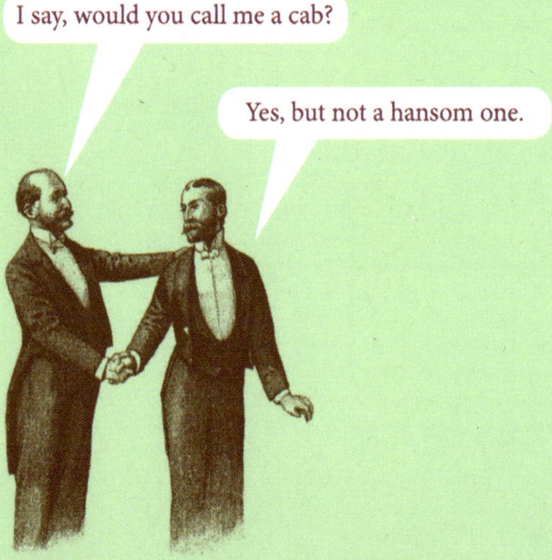
I say, would you call me a cab?
Yes, but not a hansom one.

August 2025

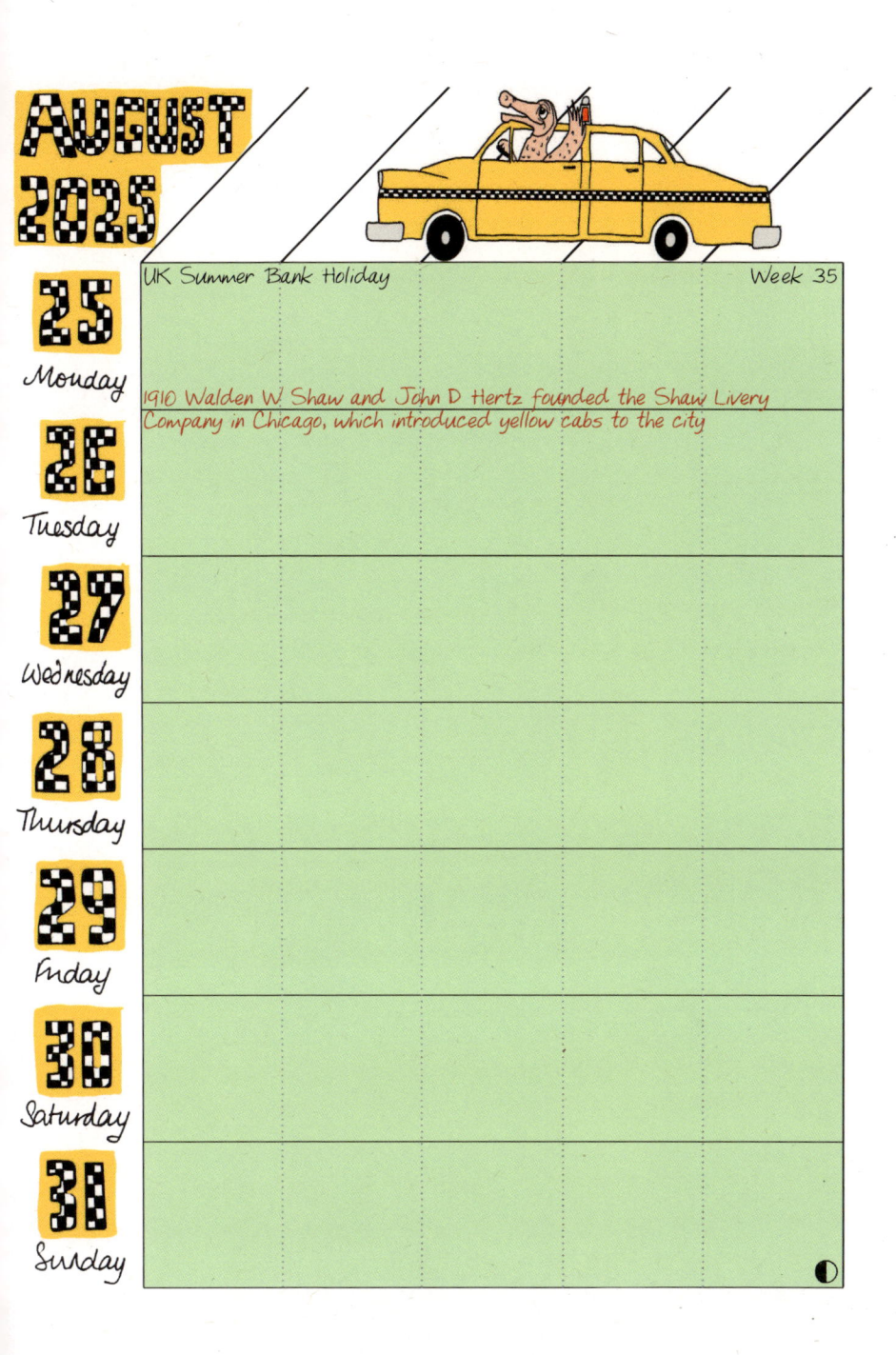

Week 35

25 Monday — UK Summer Bank Holiday

1910 Walden W Shaw and John D Hertz founded the Shaw Livery Company in Chicago, which introduced yellow cabs to the city

26 Tuesday

27 Wednesday

28 Thursday

29 Friday

30 Saturday

31 Sunday

September 2025

October 2025

November 2025	December 2025
January 2026	February 2026

Forward Planner 2025-26

SEPTEMBER 2025

1 M	LABOR DAY (U.S, CAN)	17 W	
2 T		18 Th	
3 W		19 F	
4 Th		20 S	
5 F		21 Su	
6 S		22 M	
7 Su	FATHER'S DAY (AUS)	23 T	ROSH HASHANAH
8 M		24 W	HERITAGE DAY (SA)
9 T		25 Th	
10 W		26 F	
11 Th		27 S	
12 F		28 Su	
13 S		29 M	
14 Su		30 T	
15 M			
16 T			

OCTOBER 2025

1 W		17 F	
2 Th	YOM KIPPUR	18 S	
3 F		19 Su	
4 S		20 M	DIWALI
5 Su		21 T	
6 M		22 W	
7 T		23 Th	
8 W		24 F	
9 Th		25 S	
10 F		26 Su	BST ENDS (UK)
11 S		27 M	HOLIDAY (IRE)
12 Su		28 T	
13 M	COLUMBUS DAY (US) THANKSGIVING (CAN)	29 W	
14 T		30 Th	
15 W		31 F	HALLOWE'EN
16 Th			

NOVEMBER 2025

1 S		17 M	
2 Su		18 T	
3 M		19 W	
4 T		20 Th	
5 W	GUY FAWKES' NIGHT	21 F	
6 Th		22 S	
7 F		23 Su	
8 S		24 M	
9 Su	REMEMBRANCE SUNDAY (UK)	25 T	
10 M		26 W	
11 T	VETERANS' DAY (US) REMEMBRANCE DAY (CAN)	27 Th	THANKSGIVING (US)
12 W		28 F	
13 Th		29 S	
14 F		30 Su	
15 S			
16 Su			

DECEMBER 2025

1 M		17 W	
2 T		18 Th	
3 W		19 F	
4 Th		20 S	
5 F		21 Su	
6 S		22 M	
7 Su		23 T	
8 M		24 W	
9 T		25 Th	CHRISTMAS DAY
10 W		26 F	BOXING DAY (UK, AUS, NZ) ST STEPHEN'S DAY (IRE)
11 Th		27 S	
12 F		28 Su	
13 S		29 M	
14 Su		30 T	
15 M	HANUKKAH	31 W	
16 T	DAY OF RECONCILIATION (SA)		

JANUARY 2026

1 Th	NEW YEAR'S DAY (UK, IRE, US, SA, AUS & NZ)	17 S	
2 F	BANK HOLIDAY (SCOT)	18 Su	
3 S		19 M	MARTIN LUTHER KING DAY (US)
4 Su		20 T	
5 M		21 W	
6 T		22 Th	
7 W		23 F	
8 Th		24 S	
9 F		25 Su	BURNS' NIGHT
10 S		26 M	AUSTRALIA DAY
11 Su		27 T	
12 M		28 W	
13 T		29 Th	
14 W		30 F	
15 Th		31 S	
16 F			

FEBRUARY 2026

1 Su		17 T	CHINESE NEW YEAR, SHROVE TUESDAY, RAMADAN BEGINS
2 M	ST. BRIGID'S DAY HOLIDAY (IRE)	18 W	
3 T		19 Th	
4 W		20 F	
5 Th		21 S	
6 F	WAITANGI DAY (NZ)	22 Su	
7 S		23 M	
8 Su		24 T	
9 M		25 W	
10 T		26 Th	
11 W		27 F	
12 Th		28 S	
13 F			
14 S			
15 Su			
16 M	PRESIDENTS' DAY (US)		

Public Holidays et al.
This information is correct at time of going to press. The publishers can accept no responsibility for any errors

CHINESE NEW YEAR
SHROVE TUESDAY
RAMADAN BEGINS

Where Religious Holidays are indicated, the first full day of the holiday is shown.

Forward Planner 2025-26

MARCH 2026

1 Su		17 T	
2 M		18 W	
3 T		19 Th	
4 W		20 F	
5 Th		21 S	HUMAN RIGHTS DAY (SA)
6 F		22 Su	
7 S		23 M	
8 Su		24 T	
9 M	CANBERRA DAY (AUS) COMMONWEALTH DAY	25 W	
10 T		26 Th	
11 W		27 F	
12 Th		28 S	
13 F		29 Su	BST BEGINS
14 S		30 M	
15 Su	MOTHERING SUNDAY (UK, IRE)	31 T	
16 M			

APRIL 2026

1 W		17 F	
2 Th	PASSOVER	18 S	
3 F	GOOD FRIDAY	19 Su	
4 S		20 M	
5 Su	EASTER SUNDAY	21 T	
6 M	EASTER MONDAY	22 W	
7 T		23 Th	
8 W		24 F	
9 Th		25 S	
10 F		26 Su	
11 S		27 M	ANZAC DAY (AUS, NZ) FREEDOM DAY (SA)
12 Su		28 T	
13 M		29 W	
14 T		30 Th	
15 W			
16 Th			

MAY 2026

1 F	INTERNATIONAL WORKERS' DAY (SA)	17 Su	
2 S		18 M	VICTORIA DAY (CAN)
3 Su		19 T	
4 M	MAY BANK HOLIDAY (UK, IRE)	20 W	
5 T		21 Th	
6 W		22 F	
7 Th		23 S	
8 F		24 Su	
9 S		25 M	SPRING BANK HOLIDAY (UK) MEMORIAL DAY (US)
10 Su	MOTHER'S DAY (US, SA, AUS)	26 T	
11 M		27 W	EID AL-ADHA
12 T		28 Th	
13 W		29 F	
14 Th		30 S	
15 F		31 Su	
16 S			

JUNE 2026

1 M	JUNE HOLIDAY (IRE)	17 W	ISLAMIC NEW YEAR
2 T		18 Th	
3 W		19 F	
4 Th		20 S	FATHER'S DAY (UK, US, SA, CAN)
5 F		21 Su	
6 S		22 M	
7 Su		23 T	
8 M		24 W	
9 T		25 Th	
10 W		26 F	
11 Th		27 S	
12 F		28 Su	
13 S		29 M	
14 Su		30 T	
15 M			
16 T	YOUTH DAY (SA)		

JULY 2026

1 W	CANADA DAY	17 F	
2 Th		18 S	
3 F	INDEPENDENCE DAY (US)	19 Su	
4 S		20 M	
5 Su		21 T	
6 M		22 W	
7 T		23 Th	
8 W		24 F	
9 Th		25 S	
10 F		26 Su	
11 S		27 M	
12 Su		28 T	
13 M	PUBLIC HOLIDAY (N. IRELAND)	29 W	
14 T	BASTILLE DAY	30 Th	
15 W		31 F	
16 Th			

AUGUST 2026

1 S		17 M	
2 Su		18 T	
3 M	SUMMER BANK HOLIDAY (SCOTLAND, IRE)	19 W	
4 T		20 Th	
5 W		21 F	
6 Th		22 S	
7 F		23 Su	
8 S		24 M	
9 Su	NATIONAL WOMEN'S DAY (SA)	25 T	
10 M		26 W	
11 T		27 Th	
12 W		28 F	
13 Th		29 S	
14 F		30 Su	
15 S		31 M	SUMMER BANK HOLIDAY (UK)
16 Su			

The Appendix

starts here

APPENDIX

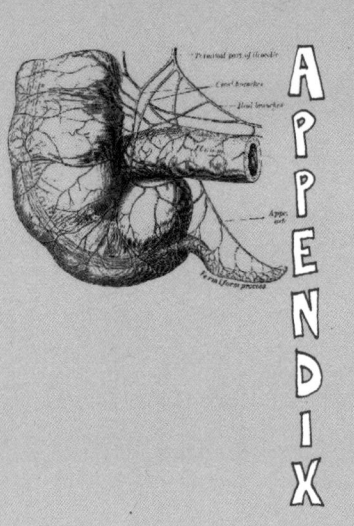

Appendix

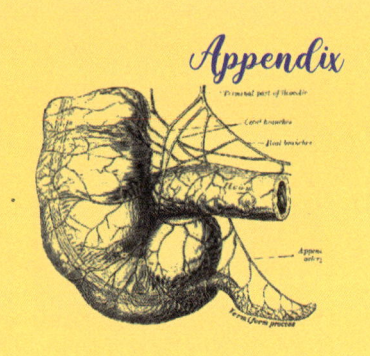

APPENDIX

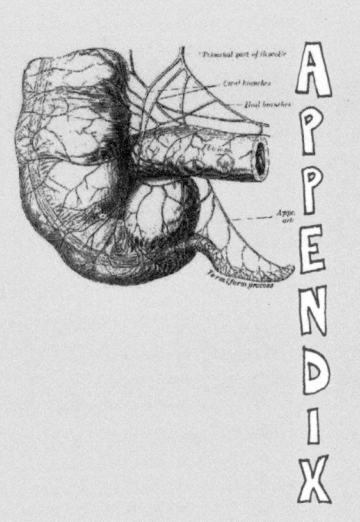

Lord Dodo Presents

FREE
DODO DOWNLOADS

The Dodo font to elevate your emails and pep up your Powerpoints

Customise your Dodo Pad or Notebook with Print, Cut and Paste Yourself stickers, designs and planning pages

Digitised content from the Dodo Towers Archive, where you can travel in a time machine to see Dodo Pads of old…

And more…go to **dodopad.com/downloads**

New items are being added all the time, so sign up for the latest news at

dodopad.com/signup

and of course

DODO DIARY PRODUCE

DODO PAD COVERS

DODO PAD NOTEBOOKS

JOTTERS

DODO PAD BOOK FOR COOKS

DODO ACCESSORIES

dodopad.com/shop